The Elder Chinese

Eva Cheng

With the Assistance of
Gladys Hom
Mary Jean Hong

Center on Aging, San Diego State University

The Elder Chinese

A CROSS-CULTURAL STUDY OF MINORITY ELDERS IN SAN DIEGO

Editor & Project Director:	Ramón Valle, PhD
Project Director:	James Ajemian, PhD (First Year)
Associate Editor:	Charles Martinez, MSW
Secretaries:	Mrs. Peggy King
	Mrs. Patricia Murphy
	Mrs. Alicia Nevarez-Krotky
	Ms. Cynthia Wright
Cover:	Mr. Calvin Woo, Humangraphics
Published By:	Center on Aging
	School of Social Work
	San Diego State University
Design Style & Phototypeset:	Betty R. Truitt
	Word Processing Center
	San Diego State University

Monographs and Technical Reports Series

The Elder American Indian:	Frank Dukepoo, PhD
The Elder Black:	E. Percil Stanford, PhD
The Elder Chinese:	Ms. Eva Cheng, MSSW
The Elder Guamanian:	Wesley H. Ishikawa, DSW
The Elder Japanese:	Ms. Karen C. Ishizuka, MSW
The Elder Latino:	Ramón Valle, PhD
	Ms. Lydia Mendoza, MS
The Elder Pilipino:	Ms. Roberta Peterson, MSSW
The Elder Samoan:	Wesley H. Ishikawa, DSW

Project Supported by Funds from U.S. Department of Health, Education and Welfare, Office of Human Development, Administration on Aging. Grant Number AoA-90-A-317, Mr. David Dowd, Project Officer AoA, OHD, DHEW.

Distributed by The Campanile Press, San Diego State University

Library of Congress Cataloging Data
Catalog Card No.: 77-83484
Cheng, Eva
The Elder Chinese
San Diego, Calif.: Campanile Press
p. 54
7708   770708

ISBN 0-916304-35-3

Distributed for the Center on Aging by
The Campanile Press
San Diego State University
5300 Campanile Drive
San Diego, California
92182

Acknowledgments

The research team extends grateful acknowledgment to the many individuals in the San Diego Chinese community who played both major and minor roles in the conduct of this project.

There are also a number of other persons who have had varying degrees of impact to the project as a whole from the proposal stage to the end. Dr. Gideon Horowitz was instrumental in developing the proposal for which initial funds were received. Dr. James Ajemian assumed the directorship for the project during its first year. Mr. Charles Martinez provided extremely helpful technical support throughout the process of the research, especially at the point of finalizing the monographs. Dr. Roger Cunniff, Mrs. Sharon Swinscoe and Mr. Gerald Thiebolt of The Campanile Press were most helpful in extending their assistance throughout the process of publishing this editorial serial of reports. The researchers are equally appreciative of the continual support from the Administration on Aging by Mr. David Dowd, Project Director. We wish also to recognize the School of Social Work of San Diego State University under whose general auspices the study was conducted.

We are grateful to all of the above for their involvement in this research effort.

/E. Cheng

Table of Contents

I. INTRODUCTION TO THE STUDY*

Research Objectives

This study of Chinese elders was undertaken as an integral part of a larger Cross-Cultural Study of Minority Elders of San Diego County. The study as a whole, extended over a two-year period, 1974-1976, and was funded by the Administration on Aging. In addition to Chinese, seven other populations of minority elders were encompassed within the research. These included, American Indian, black, Guamanian, Japanese, Latino, Pilipino, and Samoan elders, age 50 years or more. While the age designation might appear somewhat arbitrary, the half-century mark in chronological age was seen as encompassing the concept of elder as denoted within the study.

The research was undertaken with three specific objectives in mind:

- First, to analyze characteristic lifestyles and customs, as well as the primary interactional networks of ethnic minority groups and in this case, especially those of Chinese elders.
- Second, to explore and delineate the perceptions and viewpoints of the Chinese elders toward formal programmatic assistance and human service networks with the overall intent of tracing, where possible, the interactions between the formal programs and the primary networks.
- Third, to test out a methodology appropriate to obtaining information about ethnic minority populations and specifically the elders of these populations.

To a large extent, the third objective guided the total study. From the standpoint of the researchers, the methodology to be utilized was deemed extremely critical to the actual information obtained. The rationale for giving priority consideration to the research approach was twofold. It was grounded first in the researchers' previous data-gathering experiences in their respective ethnic communities, both within and outside San Diego. These experiences had provided information about the importance of such factors as providing for community relations when engaged in ethnic minority survey research efforts with ethnic minority populations. The reasoning for this approach was also based on the call for fresh research approaches both from minority social scientists, Romano (1969), Vaca (1970), Hamilton (1973), Murase (1972), Takagi (1973), as well as from ethnic majority investigators, Clark and Anderson (1967), Blauner (1973), and Moore (1973).

Study Populations

A predominant theme within the above collectivity of social investigators is the call for the utilization of what Myers (1974) has termed unconventional research approaches which, in effect, blend traditional survey research techniques with newer considerations. A major step in the direction of this methodological approach was the determination to seek a purposive, rather than statistically

---

* This methodological statement is authored by a group of researchers at the Center on Aging. With minor variations, it appears as the introductory chapter to the monographs on elder blacks, Chinese, Guamanians, Pilipinos, and Samoans, in the series, A Cross-Cultural Study of Minority Elders in San Diego.

proportionate representation of the ethnic groups. The overriding research intent was to obtain representation of ethnic life process content within the larger San Diego environment.

The San Diego environment.

The study was conducted within the County of San Diego which is also designated as a Complete Standard Metropolitan Statistical Area (SMSA) within the Bureau of Census. The total SMSA encompasses approximately 4,296 square miles and an estimated 1.5 million persons. To the south, it borders Baja California and the Mexican city of Tijuana. Orange County forms the northern border to the SMSA with the Los Angeles metropolitan complex then being immediately adjacent. To a large extent San Diego forms the nexus of a well-traveled commercial corridor stretching some 200 miles from Los Angeles to Ensenada in Baja California.

The San Diego area has an extensive military complex which serves as a base of operations for the United States Navy in several capacities including port and air facilities. The SMSA has a highly urbanized core, but is equally highly suburban. At the same time, large portions of the County are rural and sparsely populated. For example, nineteen American Indian tribes reside in rural reservations in the SMSA. There is considerable agriculture in the area wherein large numbers of persons of Mexican and Pilipino backgrounds are employed. The North County area of San Diego contains smaller cities with concentrated mixes of urban and rural populations.

Elders in San Diego.

At the initiation of the study, the researchers had varying estimates of the elderly population of the SMSA and opted to utilize the San Diego County Area Agency on Aging, 1975 projections based on the age 60-plus population. Of the total San Diego population, 1.5 million, approximately 198,300 or 13.2 percent were designated as 60-plus years. (See Table 1)

Table   1

San Diego SMSA Age 60-Plus Population Estimates

$N = 1,500,000$

Population age	f	%
Under 60 years	1,302,000	86.8
Over 60 years	198,300	13.2

SOURCE: San Diego County Area Agency on Aging, formerly the Office of Senior Citizen Affairs, updated 1975 estimates.

Of these estimated 198,300 elderly, approximately 23,900 (11.9 percent) have been classified as ethnic-minority elders, age 60 years or more (see Table 2). It must be noted, though, that the data regarding the elderly in San Diego were representations of the best estimates and projections available at the point of conducting the research.

The data regarding the ethnic elderly have been found to be in disarray due to repeated undercounts and mislabeling of ethnicity (*Counting the Forgotten,* 1974).

Table 2
San Diego SMSA Age 60-Plus
Population Estimates By Ethnic Groups

Group	f	Percent of Total Age 60-Plus Population N = 198,300	Percent of Minority 60-Plus Population By Ethnic Minority Group n = 23,900*
Anglo/ White	174,400	87.9	
Latino	14,900	7.5	62.3
Black	4,500	2.2	18.8
Pilipino	1,300	0.6	5.4
Japanese	700	0.4	2.9
American Indian	500	0.3	2.0
Chinese	300	0.2	1.4
Samoan	300	0.2	1.4
Guamanian	200	0.1	0.8
Other ethnic minorities not clearly designated	1,200	0.6	5.0

* NOTE: The Area Agency on Aging estimates of specific ethnic minority populations have been further updated with best estimates available from organizations serving each population.

As can be seen from Table 2, Latinos account for almost two-thirds (62.3 percent) of the estimated total group of minority group elderly in the San Diego area.

The Chinese study population.

A cost analysis of available project funds and time, as well as the methodology to be utilized, indicated that a study population of approximately 600 total subjects would be feasible. In fact, 628 ethnic minority persons were interviewed. Table 3 summarizes the Cross-Cultural Study population by specific ethnic designation. The further heterogeneity of each specific minority group studied along with the principal findings are described within the series of monographs commissioned through the research project.

As can be seen, despite the fact that the Chinese elderly comprise approximately 1.4 percent of all the estimated minority elderly in San Diego, they formed nearly 7.9 percent of the total study population.

Here again, the research intent intervened. To have proceeded with population sampling on a ratio or numerically proportionate basis would have meant that the Latino sample would have taken an undue amount of the study group's time, such as to preclude obtaining representative content from the other ethnic minorities.

The earlier noted disarray of demographic indicator on minority groups was also a contributing factor for the research decision to seek purposive representativeness.

Table 3

AoA Study Population

N = 628

Group	f	%
Latino	218	34.7
Black	101	16.1
Pilipino	74	11.8
American Indian	62	9.8
Japanese	60	9.6
Chinese	50	7.9
Samoan	40	6.4
Guamanian	23	3.7

The Cross-Cultural Research Group

Each ethnic minority group had a complement of university-based researchers who acted as coordinators and community-based interviewers in numbers adequate to the size of the ethnic cohort included in the study. A research decision appropriate to the methodology had indicated that researchers of the same ethnicity would operate within their respective cohorts. This strategy permitted the tailoring of the research instruments and contact patterns specifically to the linguistic and situational differentials to be encountered within each ethnic cohort. Specifically this approach allowed the translation of the interview guides into the idiom appropriate to the ethnic group to be studied.

Fortunately, the concept of providing for a match between the ethnicity of the researcher and study population had been built into the original proposal and budget, although, not in the fineline detail as necessitated at the point of actual implementation. In its totality, the research group numbered ten university-based and twenty-eight community-based interviewers who had the support of one full-time technical assistant and three clerical staff.

II. METHODOLOGY

Overview

The research strategy utilized within the inquiry was based on the theoretical perspective of combining quantitative and qualitative research approaches so that the information obtained from close-ended questions would be placed in the context of the social environment of the respondent. The theoretical sets utilized in the research stem from Glazer and Strauss (1967), Campbell and Stanley (1963), Gouldner (1965), and Sieber (1973), who collectively propose alternative considerations for survey research. In addition, the direction for the research was drawn from Myers (1974) and Valle (1974), whose empirical research demonstrated approaches toward combining both quantitative and qualitative analysis.

Figure 1 highlights the data collection strategy. If the research approach could be summarized, it could be said to have been geared to the collection of what Cooley (1908) and other theorists have termed primary group behaviors against the backdrop of complex secondary social environments. With regard to the San Diego SMSA, these include mixes of ethnically different populations living in urbanized as well as dispersed and ruralized situations and all living in an equally complex network of systems and services. The questions asked by the researchers centered then both on obtaining indicators of ethnicity and primary behaviors in the context of their secondary group and interactional environments.

Figure   1
Overall Strategy for Data Collection

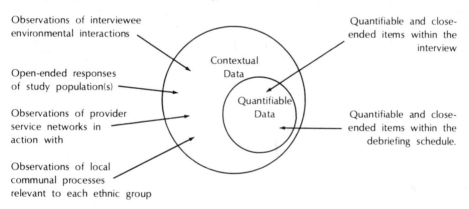

In operational terms, the methodology deployed within the study encompassed a series of lockstep phases and planned sequential interactions beginning with community involvement.

Community Consultation and Dissemination Network

A key ingredient to the total research effort was the development and maintenance of a multilevel pattern of interaction with varied constituencies from each of the ethnic minority groups throughout the life of the study. To some extent, the rationale for this mode also arose from the expressed reluctance early in 1974 of various minority constituencies to have more university researchers traipsing through their communities, even though the researchers might be ethnics themselves. This process though, had been anticipated by the researchers before word of the proposed research was allowed to circulate throughout the broader community.

In setting up the contact network, each coordinator was made responsible for the formal and informal interfacing with his or her ethnic group constituencies. The process was designed to be continuously open throughout the life of the study. It was expected that some of the constituencies would not or could not become involved at the beginning of the process. Either some constituencies were unknown to the researchers, or they would not become informed until sometime after the project was well underway. In this manner, any of the constituent groups desiring information and access to the research could secure what was available at whatever point in time they entered the process.

It should be noted that as time permitted, a like pattern of open interaction was maintained with constituencies other than the ethnic minorities and included other researchers, both within San Diego and in other cities, to include persons significantly involved in the field of aging.

As envisioned by the researchers, the benefits of this process far outweighed the time expenditure drawbacks in that the continuous interaction facilitated obtaining of the project interviewers as well as the study subjects. Moreover, the maintenance of this ongoing contact has, at the point of termination of the project, provided the project with a built-in dissemination network of interested individuals who could directly address the findings of the inquiry. In keeping with this intent, each of the research coordinators filed his or her dissemination plan at the end of the project, in order to coordinate dissemination activity beyond the expiration of project funds.

Population Selection

The study cohort was selected on the basis of attempting to tap into the normal or ordinary relational patterns of the ethnic populations targeted to be included within the study. Initial selection was therefore based on lists of potential respondents obtained from the several constituencies to which the researchers were already linked. In many instances, this meant that the initial selection included a number of persons who formally belonged to ethnic organizations. From that point, allowance was made for individuals to be included in the study on the basis of referrals from some of the interviewees themselves, as well as from other community persons, once the interviewer had obtained credibility either in a particular neighborhood or interactional linkage network. With conscious intent, the population selection process was designed to include brokering persons who often served as connectors between the interviewer and the potential interviewee. These brokering or contact persons could be translators, community volunteers or agency workers, or simply key neighborhood leaders.

Interviewer Selection and Training

The community consultation process as designed also provided the vehicle whereby the university-based researchers could obtain a cadre of potential interviewers. The ongoing contact with the community was such as to allow both the university-based researchers and prospective community-based interviewers to prescreen each other. In practice, the four-month period of November 1974 through to February 1975, was allotted to this purpose. As a consequence, when the training period began in March of 1975, a preselected group of interviewers was available from all of the respective ethnic groups.

The formal training for the interviewers encompassed twenty-eight hours. The interviewers were trained both as a total group and within their respective ethnic group where individualized concerns about language, customs, and interview style were emphasized. The first two interviews per interviewer were made part of the training process and all interviewers were debriefed intensively to reinforce the training as to fine tune the methodology.

Throughout the training, the interviewers were encouraged to proceed with their own natural styles. It should be noted that the community interaction had acted as a screening process and had attracted individuals who were experienced either as volunteers or agency aides. In some instances, several came to the study with prior formal research interviewing experience on other projects. The overall training intent was to free the interviewers to augment their own natural and culturally appropriate capabilities while at the same time, furnishing them with the necessary data collection and recording techniques.

In the second year of the project, the interviewers were invited to join in the analysis, as well as participate in the documentation of the findings in a continued part-time paid capacity. The interviewers also joined in the dissemination efforts of the project.

Interview Strategy

The plática research methodology (Valle, 1974), combined with the "unconventional survey research approach," (Myers, 1974), as utilized throughout the total study has several distinguishing features. First, the interview is seen as an interaction which has all the trappings of a beginning interpersonal relationship (Stebbins, 1972). Second, the strategy builds upon an open discussion approach wherein the interview proceeds in the format of building trust and confidence on a conversational and mutual exchange basis. Third, within this kind of interviewing, the research focus is first on all of the human exchange aspects and only then on the information to be obtained. Fourth, the maintenance of the relationship-oriented conversational approach is seen as continuous throughout the total interview. Fifth, the strategy includes the incorporation of observational techniques (Sieber, 1972), wherein the interviewer observes the living surroundings and environmental interactions of the interviewee. By design the interviews were seen as taking place in the interviewee's home. Sixth, at all points of the interview, the interviewer secures the consent of the interviewee to obtain information on an ongoing basis as appropriate throughout the interview process. The interviewer is mandated to be especially sensitive to obtain consent to more sensitive personal information areas and to provide the option to the interviewee either to refuse to answer or to terminate the interview. The culturally syntonic (appropriate) clues, both verbal and affective, which comprise the core of this approach were worked out in the training period, as well as in the debriefing.

With regard to the notion of informed consent, it should be noted that the study was initiated prior to the promulgation of the Department of Health, Education, and Welfare human subject research guidelines *Federal Register* (1975). The informed consent procedures utilized within the study did conform to the option of modified procedures wherein the written consent of the interviewee is not required but respondent's rights to privacy and refusal to participate are clearly protected. The best advice of the project's community consultants and interviewers had indicated that the Guamanian elders' apprehension might well be increased rather than decreased by having to sign consent forms.

The Interview Instrument

The interview instrument was designed to be utilized as a guide for information collection within specific categories. This approach was selected on the basis of the diversity of the languages (and dialects) represented within the study populations. For example, the Chinese population group represented a number of the Chinese dialects, to include, Cantonese and Mandarin. Within the Pilipino group, several provincial languages were represented, including Tagalog and Ilocano. In practice, this meant that the field researchers utilized a basic interview instrument containing questions grouped around sixteen major variable categories congruent with the stated research objectives of the inquiry.

An illustration might assist in clarifying the instrument design. A key item of information for the study was obtaining the respondent's age. Among some of the ethnic groups, Latinos and Japanese in particular, it is culturally rude to ask another's age directly. More circumspect behaviors are required, for example, first obtaining the place of birth and then requesting permission to record the date. This meant also that in some cases, the dates were provided in terms of other than the Occidental calendar. In these instances, the responses were given in terms of significant events which had taken place within the ethnic minority group history. For example, being born at the point of a major immigration by a whole village to the United States. The selection of interviewers then focused on their ability to move easily between the standard interview data to be obtained and the cultural nuances attendant to the interviewee's ethnically-based responses.

In keeping with the contextual strategy of the research, the instrument contained open-ended items woven in between the close-ended questions. The interviewer often then had to phrase all of these questions in the particular local idiom. Overall, the interview was designed to be a relatively long interpersonal experience. Moveover, it was approached from the aspect that it could be a pleasant and possibly therapeutic experience for the respondent.

Data Collection Procedures

Data collection included three distinct operations: the interview itself, recording of the data and debriefing.

The interview process.

While variations in the interview style were allowed, a general pattern was established in training. This involved developing a set of interview behaviors deemed appropriate, such as establishing precontacts in the mode acceptable to specific ethnic groups. These precontacts could range from a written letter or a phone call through to having a cultural broker intercede in order to establish the interview. During the interview itself, the field researchers were free to accept food and drink as deemed appropriate and to vary the interview length and intensity also as appropriate. By predetermination, all interviewees were paid an honorarium of ten dollars for their time and effort, regardless of length or completeness of the interview. The honorarium was not announced beforehand, but provided at the end of the interview. The rationale for the payment to interviewees emerged from the several ethnic constituencies whose members were advising the research project. In their collective thinking the ten dollars represented an in-kind exchange to the interviewee for his or her time and information.

Data collection.

Data was collected at all points of the interview. The interviewers were encouraged to record open-ended responses in as much detail as possible and in the language of the respondents. The interviewers also were equally encouraged to record any open-ended additions given in the context of any close-ended item, as it would be elicited in the course of the interview. A common illustration might serve to highlight the process. In many instances, the above-noted request for the close-ended date of birth would often elicit open-ended discussion around the early life experiences of the respondent.

In terms of recording style, the interviewers were left free to record information during the interview and/or after the interview itself, depending on respondent's comfortableness with the situation, as well as depending upon the procedures as acceptable by each ethnic group. This approach was also designed to accommodate the information storage style of the interviewer. Some were more comfortable writing during the interview, some more so immediately after. A general capability among the interviewer group was their skill in the area of retaining and reporting back oral history-type process which was tested out during the training stage of the research.

Debriefing.

In the actual working out of the research, the interviewers were debriefed according to various modes. These included debriefings on an interview by interview basis, as well as debriefings encompassing the interviewer's total sample. The debriefing intent was to collect as much contextual data regarding each interview as possible as well as to obtain as much descriptive information surrounding what might be considered the more open-ended items within the guide. Debriefings were conducted by the university-based coordinators. A debriefing schedule complete with close-ended coded items was developed for the research.

Data Analysis

The analysis of the data was seen as a mesh of both quantitative and qualitative approaches. With regard to the quantitative data, the Statistical Package for Social Sciences (SPSS) computer program format was employed. For the purposes of the monograph level of reporting, frequency distributions and percentages were seen as the most appropriate statistical format. For purposes of the major project report which compares intergroup variables, statistical measures including analysis of variance and factor analysis were seen as applicable. In all instances, the quantitative analysis was to be played against the backdrop of the ethnic-environmental context in which it was obtained.

The process of analysis was seen as being relatively long in duration, consuming most of the second year of the project. During this phase, the interviewers joined the university-based researchers as fellow analysts and assisted in conceptualizing and interpreting the findings, as well as in instances, assisting in writing portions of the final monograph products.

Expected Outcomes

The expected outcomes of the research were cast in terms of the three principal study objectives: to trace the respective cultural patterns of the ethnically varied study population; to delineate the respondents' outlooks toward formal services and networks of services; and to test an alternative data gathering methodology.

It was expected that the study, as a whole, including this series of monographs, would provide findings to impact the field of aging at four levels: (a) direct services and programs for ethnic elders, (b) policies affecting minority seniors, (c) the training of professionals to serve in the field of aging, and (d) further research in the field of ethnicity and aging.

Methodological Considerations Specific to Chinese Sample

At the outset of the research project, contact was made with organizations serving Chinese populations in San Diego County. The purpose of the contact was twofold. First to solicit active participation from the Chinese community leadership in the projected research. Second, to develop an initial pool of referrals to serve as interviewers and interviewees for the research. As a result of preliminary contact with the community, three Chinese interviewers were selected and trained for research interviewing.

The questionnaire translated into Chinese and English was field-tested by the interviewers. Debriefing sessions with them concluded after twenty-eight hours of training.

Subsequent to the selection and training of the interviewers, the interview team proceeded to select interviewees from lists compiled by a number of Chinese churches and social service agencies in San Diego. The list included: (1) Mandarin speaking, belonging to a Mandarin church, (b) seniors attending the Chinese Church, House of China and/or Chinese Social Service Center events and (c) the socially isolated senior who did not belong to or participate in any Chinese organization. This list was reviewed by the interviewers, who then selected potential interviewees according to age (e.g., must be 55 years or older), organizational affiliation, dialect spoken and area of residence.

The contact methods utilized varied according to the interviewer. For example, one interviewer made no precontacts due to her familiarity with interviewees and the knowledge that precontact may have created suspicion due to its formal and official nature. On the other hand, the other two interviewers almost always included a telephone or personal contact in their data collection procedures. These two interviewers were assisted on the precontact phase by ministers, friends, or relatives of potential respondents.

Within the 50 interviews, the initial phases of the interview process featured an informational exchange between interviewer and interviewee and in some instances, at the outset, the interviewer was interviewed by the interviewee. Upon termination of the interview, the interviewees received ten dollars. This stipend created an element of surprise among the interviewees, and many refused to accept the fee. They viewed the interviewer's visit as a favor. Once assured that the money was being paid to all interviewees and that it was not coming from the interviewer's pocket, the interviewees accepted the money. In some instances, meals or vegetables were offered to the interviewers as a sign of the interviewee's hospitality, as well as their enjoyment and appreciation of the company of the interviewer.

After the collected data were coded and keypunched, computer runs were made for frequency distribution and percent analysis.

III. FINDINGS

A Profile of the Chinese Study Group

Age and sex distribution.

The Chinese sample included a total of 50 individuals ranging in age from 56 to 87 years. The mean age for the study sample was 70.88 years. Within the study population, 26 (52 percent) were male and 24 (48 percent) were female.

Marital status.

Of the 50 respondents, 25 (50 percent) were married and 44 percent were widowed, 2 (4 percent) were divorced and one person never married. (See Table 4.)

Table 4

Marital Status $n = 50$

Status	f	%
Married	25	50
Widowed	22	44
Divorced	2	4
Never married	1	2

Employment and Income

With regard to employment, 33 respondents (66 percent of the sample) had indicated previous employment in occupations within the food and laundry business, 11 (22 percent) noted they had never been employed in past years, 8 percent of the sample noted that their spouses had worked in the past, and 12 percent of the sample responded in a manner which was categorized as nonapplicable.

Of the 66 percent of the respondents who indicated past employment, one-third of this group (22 percent of the total Chinese sample) were currently employed either on a full-time (12 percent of sample), or part-time basis (10 percent of sample). The remaining two-thirds of persons indicating past employment (44 percent of sample) were currently retired. For those persons currently retired, their length of retirement ranged from one to more than ten years, with 38 percent of the total Chinese sample noting that they had been retired for a minimum of five years.

Of the 50 respondents, 54 percent indicated that they would prefer not to work due to poor health, old age, inability to speak English, and lack of marketable skills.

Five (10 percent) of the sample who indicated a desire to work cited occupations such as house cleaning, sewing, babysitting, and kitchen help.

With regard to income, 66 percent of the sample considered their financial situation as "fair," 22 percent viewed their situation to be "good," and 10 percent responded that their financial situation was "poor." Additionally, another 2 percent indicated they did not know if their financial situation was good, fair or poor (see Table 5). The monthly income range for the sample was from zero dollars (20 percent) to $2,000. The mean monthly income was $385 with the median level being $214.

Table 5

Financial Status of Respondents   *n* = 50

Status	*f*	%
Good	33	66
Fair	11	22
Poor	5	10
Didn't know	1	2

Principal sources of income for the sample varied from social security (50 percent of sample), wages and salaries (22 percent), SSI (2 percent), and assistance from family (8 percent). Other miscellaneous sources such as pensions, unemployment and income from persons renting property from the respondent, were 18 percent. Secondary sources of income for the sample ranged from social security (10 percent), SSI (4 percent), and wages and salaries (8 percent).

Educational level.

Seventy-five percent of the sample indicated they had some type of formal education, 22 percent did not have any and 4 percent responded that they were self-educated. Years of educational attainment ranged from zero to 20 years, with the mean being 6.8 years.

Housing patterns.

Of the 50 respondents, 34 percent owned their homes, 14 percent were in the process of buying their homes, 20 percent were renting an apartment or house, 28 percent were living with children and contributing to house payments or rent, 2 percent were not monetarily contributing to their housing and 2 percent were living in a room and board project for seniors.

For those respondents making house or rent payments, 18 persons (36 percent) paid less than $200 per month and 8 others (16 percent) paid less than $50 per month.

Language preference.

Eighty percent of the sample indicated Chinese as their first preference with 44 percent indicating English as their second language preference. Thirty percent of the sample could not speak English, 42 percent could get by speaking English, and 28 percent responded that they could get by speaking English but with some difficulty.

Origins and residency patterns.

Eighty-four percent of the sample were foreign-born with the remaining 16 percent born in the United States. Over one-half (56.8 percent) of the respondents had arrived in mainland United States at least 35 years ago, and 10 percent have been living in the United States for as long as 60 years.

Seventy percent of the respondents have resided in the San Diego area from at least ten years to no more than 63 years, with the mean years of residency in San Diego for the sample being 31 years. Additionally, 34 percent have lived at the same residence for more than 20 years and 70 percent have lived at the same residence for at least 5 years.

Needs

Health.

Of the sample, 32 persons (64 percent) considered their health as being "good," 7 (14 percent) responded that their health was "fair," and 11 (22 percent) indicated "poor" health (see Table 6).

Table 6
Health Status $n = 50$

Status	f	%
Good	32	64
Fair	7	14
Poor	11	22

In regard to the question, "What do you feel are the major reasons older people sometimes do not go to the doctor or clinic even though something is bothering them," the factors identified as major deterrents to use were: (a) financial situation, as well as high costs of medical services (38 percent), (b) lack of faith in doctors (24 percent) and (c) language barriers (i.e., no bilingual staff at medical facility) were given as reasons by 16 percent of the sample.

Minor deterrents to use of medical facilities cited by respondents included: (a) fear of illness and consequences of doctor's examination (2 percent), (b) inconvenience of going to the doctor's office (4 percent), (c) other reasons (6 percent), and (d) 10 percent of the respondents gave answers which were "not applicable," (e.g., "I see a doctor when I'm sick").

Transportation.

The automobile was singled out as the primary means of transportation by 31 (62 percent) of the respondents. The second and third most frequent means of transportation were "walking," 10 respondents (20 percent), and "public transportation, 9 respondents (18 percent). (See Table 7.)

Of the sample, 15 (30 percent) of the respondents indicated private ownership of an automobile and 28 (56 percent) responded that they had access to someone who would provide transportation when necessary.

In total, 37 (74 percent) could find some form of transportation and the remaining 13 (26 percent) could not find any form of transportation when necessary.

Table   7

Means of Transportation $n = 50$

Means	f	%
Automobile	31	62
Walking	10	20
Public transportation	9	18

Nutrition.

Twenty-six (52 percent) of the respondents reported a diet consisting of mostly ethnic foods, 42 percent responded that their diet included a mix of ethnic and non-ethnic foods, and the remaining 6 percent noted a preference for non-ethnic foods (see Table 8).

Table   8

Diet $n = 50$

Foods	f	%
Mostly ethnic	26	52
Mixed ethnic & non-ethnic	21	42
Non-ethnic	3	6

Within the total sample, 27 (54 percent) indicated that preparation of food was done by themselves, 13 (26 percent) noted that meals were prepared by spouse, 6 (12 percent) had their meals prepared by an adult neighbor and 2 (4 percent) had meals prepared by someone other than a spouse or adult neighbor.

Of the total sample, 72 percent (36 respondents) indicated that meals were eaten three times a day, 24 percent responded that meals were eaten twice a day, 2 percent ate only one meal a day and 4 percent noted that meals were eaten four or more times a day.

While 19 (38 percent) of the sample ate meals by themselves, 12 (24 percent) ate meals with one person, 11 (22 percent) participated in group meals with two to four other persons and the remaining 16 percent had their meals with five or more persons.

Interactional Coping Networks

The research also focused on attempts to map out the interviewees' natural networks and normal patterns of coping for meeting their needs. Precluding findings on these coping patterns are findings on the demographics of the sample's families.

Family.

Of the total sample, 49 (98 percent) indicated they had family. While 12 percent of the sample responded they had siblings residing within San Diego

County, an additional 21 (42 percent) had siblings living outside of San Diego County. In regard to children and grandchildren, 44 percent of the sample responded that they had children living within San Diego County and 28 percent noted they lived with their children, while 24 percent had children residing in the immediate neighborhood. Those respondents who indicated they had children residing outside of San Diego County, numbered 80 percent of the sample. Additionally, 35 (70 percent) noted that they had grandchildren residing outside San Diego County and the remaining 30 percent indicated they had grandchildren living within San Diego County. Of those indicating that grandchildren lived in San Diego County, it was further noted that the great-grandchildren or grandchildren lived in the same residence (22 percent), or in the immediate neighborhood (20 percent). Additionally, while 96 percent of the sample responded they had no other relatives living in San Diego County, 40 percent indicated they had relatives living outside of San Diego County. Contact with relatives varied from as frequent as once or more a week (13 percent), to at least once a month (32 percent), to at least once a year (13 percent). Of the total sample, 62 percent responded that they would prefer more contact with relatives, 28 percent wished to maintain their frequency of contact with relatives, 2 percent indicated a preference for less contact with relatives, and 8 percent gave answers which were "not applicable" (see Table 9).

Table   9
Contact Preference with Relatives n = 50

Preference	f	%
More contact	31	62
Same amount of contact	14	28
Less contact	1	2
Nonapplicable responses	4	8

In regard to factors which impeded contacts with relatives, the most frequent factor noted was transportation (58 percent), with other noted factors such as time (16 percent), distance (54 percent) and immigration problems (22 percent).

Helping patterns.

In regard to whom the respondent would turn first when difficulties arose, 34 (68 percent) responded that they would first turn to a family member, 5 (10 percent) indicated they would initially seek assistance from social service agencies, 4 percent would turn to a friend, 2 percent would seek the assistance of a priest, 6 percent would turn to no one but themselves, 8 percent would turn to someone other than the above mentioned groups, and the remaining 2 percent considered the question not applicable.

Regarding to whom they would turn when specific problems arose with health, 58 percent of the respondents would turn to family, 26 percent would rely on themselves for assistance, 10 percent would turn to an agency or a professional person, 2 percent would turn to a friend, and 4 percent would turn to someone other than the aforementioned groups. In regard to transportation-related problems, 52 percent would turn to their family, 18 percent responded that they would turn to themselves, 6 percent would seek assistance from a friend, 2 percent would turn to an agency or professional person, 4 percent would turn to a member of an organized group, and 18 percent would turn to someone other than the groups previously mentioned. Although 54 percent of the sample expressed no concern for minor financial problems, 34 percent indicated they relied on family for such assistance and 12 percent relied on themselves. Findings for major financial assistance indicated that 34 percent of the sample would turn to their family, 10 percent would turn to themselves, and 56 percent considered the situation as never arising. In instances necessitating assistance with physical problems, 44 percent of the respondents turned first to family, while 18 percent would rely on themselves or no one. In instances where there was a shortage of food, 12 percent of the sample would turn to the family, whereas 82 percent completely ruled out the possibility of a situation arising. When the need for counseling/talking arose, an equal number of persons, 13 (26 percent), indicated they would turn to (a) family or (b) friends, with 36 percent of the sample responding that talking/counseling was not foreseen as a need. (See Table 10.)

In all categories related to specific needs, the seeking of assistance from social service agencies and/or professional persons was almost non-existent, in that family members were noted as the primary source of assistance.

Last, of the 50 respondents, 66 percent indicated that those individuals they turned to for help resided within their immediate neighborhood and 28 percent responded that those which offered assistance were from outside of their neighborhood.

Do you help others.

When asked if the interviewees themselves provided assistance to individuals, 58 percent responded affirmatively and 42 percent indicated they did not help others. Of the 29 individuals (58 percent) who indicated they provided assistance, 9 (18 percent) helped others "often," 9 (18 percent) helped others "sometimes," and 11 (22 percent) responded that they provided "little" assistance to others.

In terms of prioritizing their assistance, first priority was given to assisting friends and neighbors (34 percent of the sample), family members (12 percent), and the church or church members (10 percent). Second priority was given to assisting family (10 percent) and the church (6 percent).

Types of assistance provided included assistance with health problems (14 percent of the sample), transportation (10 percent), chores (16 percent) and financial matters (12 percent).

Relationship to Formal Services

A general question was designed to gather data reflecting the respondents' knowledge of formal agencies or organizations which address social needs. In response to this general question, 35 (70 percent) of the sample indicated that they knew of such agencies and the remaining 15 (30 percent) responded that they had no knowledge of such agencies.

Table 10
To Whom Respondents Turn in Time of Need

| | To Whom Respondents Turn $n = 50$ | | | | | | | | | | | | | |
| Area of Need | Family | | Self/ no one | | Agency or Professional Person | | Friend | | Other | | Member Organized Group | | No Problem[1] | |
	f	%	f	%	f	%	f	%	f	%	f	%	f	%
Health	29	58	13	26	5	10	1	2	2	4				
Transportation	26	52	9	18	1	2	3	6	9	18	2	4		
Financial														
Minor	17	34	6	12									27	54
Major	17	34	5	10									28	56
Physical problems	22	44	9	18			4	8	9	18			6	12
Talking/counseling	13	26	4	8			13	26	2	4			18	36
Food shortage	6	12	2	4	1	2							41	82

1. Did not foresee as a problem or need

Further into the course of the interview, the respondents were asked if, given the need and the opportunity, had they used or were they presently using, or would they use formal human service agencies. Of the 50 respondents, 8 (18 percent) admitted they were using or had used formal agencies, 21 (42 percent) noted a willingness to utilize such agencies and 17 (34 percent) responded that they would not use formal agencies. The remaining 4 respondents (8 percent), did not foresee such situations arising and therefore declined to provide an answer.

When queried as to knowledge of specific types of categories of formal human care services, 24 (48 percent) knew about agencies providing health and medical care, 5 (10 percent) indicated knowledge of agencies addressing financial need and 8 (16 percent) knew of agencies related to nutritional needs.

In regard to knowledge and utilization of MediCal and Medicare, 34 (68 percent) and 41 (82 percent), respectively, indicated knowledge of these two programs. MediCal was utilized by 8 (16 percent) and Medicare was utilized by 23 (56 percent) of the sample. (See Table 11.)

Table 11
Knowledge and Use of MediCal/Medicare
$n = 50$

	f	%
Knew about MediCal	34	68
Utilized MediCal	8	16
Knew about Medicare	41	82
Utilized Medicare	23	56

From another perspective, the respondents were asked if they could indicate where services might be needed, but were not readily or clearly available to them. Of the 50 respondents, 21 (42 percent) did indicate a need for services which were currently unavailable.

Respondents then provided specific types of services which were in need, but not available. These specific service categories included a need for bilingual (Chinese-English) services, 11 (22 percent); outreach services, 8 (16 percent); and more social service programs (14 percent).

The respondents were then asked to provide any suggestion they might have to agencies and their personnel in regard to capabilities and style of service. Thirty-two (64 percent) of the sample indicated they had suggestions, while the remaining 36 percent did not have any comment. Specific suggestions from the 32 respondents included a need for agency personnel to have: (a) bilingual capabilities, 18 (36 percent); (b) knowledge of Chinese culture, 2 (4 percent); (c) knowledge of lifestyle and needs of population served, 11 (22 percent); and (d) courtesy and patience in working with persons, 8 (16 percent).

Aspects of Life Satisfaction

Life is better/worse.

An attempt was made by the researchers to look into the respondents' perceptions of aspects of life satisfaction.

In regard to the general question of, "Do you think things in general are getting better, the same, or worse for Chinese," 17 (34 percent) viewed things as getting better. Of the total sample, 18 (36 percent) indicated things were getting worse and 8 (16 percent) responded that things were the same. The remaining 7 interviewees did not respond to the question. (See Table 12.)

Table 12
Life Satisfaction $n = 50$

	f	%
Life is better	17	34
Life is same	8	16
Life is worse	18	36
No response	7	14

General responses given by individuals noting "things are getting better," included less racial discrimination (16 percent), increased educational and economic opportunities (16 percent), and a higher standard of living for the Chinese (8 percent). Comments offered by respondents as to why "things are getting worse," included crime (10 percent, inflation (6 percent), and 18 percent indicated that the Americanization of the younger Chinese is disturbing in that it is seen as attributing to the youth's lack of (a) available time and (b) respect for the older Chinese person. Additionally, with 13 (26 percent) of the respondents, the question generated ambivalence as reflected in the response that "some things are better, some are worse, as I hear about or see them in others."

Neighborhood.

With regard to feelings about their immediate neighborhood, 43 (86 percent) of the sample noted they were satisfied with their present neighborhood, 8 percent indicated it was fair and the remaining 6 percent rated their neighborhood as "poor." Determinants of a good neighborhood as noted by respondents (some respondents rated more than one determinant) included: (a) comfort and security (52 percent), (b) good neighbors (60 percent), (c) closeness to family and ethnic friends (36 percent), (d) closeness to resources (34 percent) and (e) environment and weather conducive to good health (10 percent).

Although 86 percent of the sample were satisfied with their immediate neighborhood, when queried if they would consider moving from their neighborhood, 15 (30 percent) answered affirmatively. Reasons cited for moving included loneliness due to lack of friends or family in the neighborhood (22 percent), as well as vandalism (8 percent). The remaining 35 (70 percent) who indicated they would not move, cited reasons such as safety and convenience (26 percent), closeness to family and friends (26 percent) and emotional attachment to home where they have resided for a lengthy period of time (18 percent).

Activities

Of the 50 respondents, 33 (66 percent) were members of an organized group. Within this subgroup of 33 respondents who indicated group membership, 20 noted affiliation with religious clubs, 11 noted membership in ethnic-social organizations and the remaining 2 respondents belonged to a work-related organization. Of these 33, 12 individuals noted affiliation with more than one organization. These affiliations included ethnic-social organizations, 9 respondents (18 percent of sample); religious organization, 1 (2 percent); and recreational groups, 2 (4 percent).

With regard to ethnic composition of organizations, 48 of the respondents (96 percent), indicated membership in organizations comprised solely of Chinese and 9 (18 percent) responded that their organization contained a mixed ethnic membership. With regard to the 12 respondents who indicated affiliation with more than one organization, 9 (18 percent of the sample) belonged to groups comprised solely of Chinese and 3 (6 percent) indicated membership in groups comprised of a mixed ethnic composition.

Activities engaged in by the study sample included gardening, relaxing at home, reading, television, and arts and crafts, 22 (44 percent); as well as walking around, 8 (16 percent); and doing something with friends, 20 (40 percent). For 44 respondents (88 percent), activities were done mostly alone. The remaining respondents engaged in activities with family (8 percent) or friends (2 percent).

As a second preference, activities were engaged in with friends (22 percent), family (12 percent) and organized groups (18 percent).

In regard to religious affiliation, 46 percent indicated adherence to a religious group.

With regard to ethnicity of friends, 70 percent of the respondents were a part of a friendship group comprised solely of Chinese, 22 percent belonged to friendship groups which were comprised of a mixed ethnic group, 6 percent indicated that their friendship group was non-ethnic in composition, and 2 percent responded that they did not belong to a friendship group.

With regard to celebrating festive occasions, 70 percent celebrated some ethnic, religious and/or national occasions. Of the total sample 52 percent observed mostly ethnic occasions. Family gatherings were also celebrated.

Most of the interviewees celebrated the ethnic festivals by sharing a big ethnic meal with family and friends. Special food for the festival would also be prepared. Participation in the cultural celebrations held by ethnic groups or church would also take place. Family celebrations such as births and birthdays included big dinners, special food and/or picnics with families and friends.

Concept of Aging

In regard to the question, "What do you think determines when a person is considered old?" 21 (42 percent) cited chronological age as the determining factor, 13 (26 percent) viewed one's physical and mental conditions, 12 percent regarded oldness as a state of mind, 6 percent indicated dependency on others, and 10 percent considered the inability to continue working as a sign of old age. It should be noted that none of the respondents indicated appearance or loss of respect as determinants of old age.

Recommendations for Meeting Needs

The study design included a question regarding the elders' perception of what can be done to meet existing needs and who should be responsible. Of the 50 respondents, a majority (54 percent), noted the government should be responsible for addressing needs with other responses indicating a local Chinese social agency (6 percent), and members of the Chinese community who were knowledgeable of existing needs (30 percent).

In regard to specific responses around (a) housing and (b) income, 6 respondents (12 percent) indicated that the government should build housing for Chinese seniors and a significant proportion of the sample (46 percent) noted that the government should increase cash payments or supportive services (e.g., low cost senior housing).

Methodological Findings

The following are descriptive data and debriefing impressions of the precontact, travel time, recording and debriefing phases of the research.

Precontact.

Some form of precontact was made with 48 (96 percent) of the respondents. Of the total sample, 37 (74 percent) required one precontact by the interviewer or a mutual friend of the interviewer and interviewee. The remaining 11 persons (22 percent) required two precontact visits prior to the actual interview.

Interview.

In regard to language of the interview, 35 (70 percent) of the interviews were predominantly conducted in Chinese, with the remaining 15 (30 percent) in English. Three of the 35 interviews were conducted predominantly in Chinese and were also partly carried out in English, and 5 of the 15 "English" interviews were partly conducted in Chinese. Thus, in essence 32 (64 percent) of the interviews were conducted solely in Chinese, 10 (20 percent) were conducted only in English and 8 (16 percent) of the interviews featured a blend of Chinese and English.

In the course of the interview, there were others present throughout the total interview in 14 cases. Others were present during some time, but not throughout the interview in 13 cases and in 23 cases no one else was present in the course of the interview.

With regard to time, 37 (74 percent) of the interviews required between one and two hours, while 10 (20 percent) lasted more than two hours.

In the course of debriefing, interviewers reported sharing information about their personal lives and background. In total, this information exchange occurred in 35 (70 percent) of the interviews.

With regard to sharing their experiences, the field researchers were also asked to explain their rationale. In approximately 30 (60 percent) of the interviews, this technique was utilized as a method of establishing trust or rapport with the interviewee.

The interviewers were also requested to guage the degree to which they had reached a state of friendliness or intimacy during the interview. In 44 (88 percent) of the interviews, it was noted by the field researchers that this friendliness and intimacy was evident throughout the interview. Of the total sample, 5 (10 percent) of the interviews were viewed as beginning formally and becoming more friendly during the course of the interview, and in one case (2 percent), the observation was that no intimacy or friendliness was established. In short, in all but one of the 50 interviews there was some state of friendliness or intimacy established.

In consultation with the project interviewers and with the community consultants, determination was made that the field researchers, at the time of the interview, could at his or her discretion, provide services to the respondent.

The training process reinforced this by providing interviewers with information and referral tickets relevant to services for the elderly. The only restraints on the activity were two. First, that the service be extended after the interview itself and specifically after the respondent had answered question 43 on the interview schedule, which related to their knowledge and use of services. Second, that the interviewers offer services in concert with the limitations of their available time and resources, as the project could in no way provide service delivery monies.

As a consequence, the field researchers extended services in approximately 28 (56 percent) of the interview situations. In the main, these services were of an informational and referral nature, but they did include a range of other activities such as linking the respondents with friends, writing and translating letters and helping with job placement.

At almost every interview, the interviewers were offered food and drinks, either as a snack or meal. Some respondents enjoyed the visit so much that they insisted that the interviewers take home some homemade or grown gifts. Others showed their trust and closeness by confiding their personal affairs in the interviewers.

Recording time.

The interviewers were requested to document their recording time for each of the interviews. In 13 (26 percent) of the interviews, recording time was less than 45 minutes, 46 to 60 minutes were required for recording in 24 (48 percent) of the interviews and in 13 (26 percent) of the interviews more than one hour was required for recording.

Travel time.

Interviewers' travel time required less than 30 minutes in 24 (48 percent) of the interviews, 15 (30 percent) required from 30 minutes to less than one hour, and the remaining 11 (22 percent) of the cases required travel time exceeding one hour.

IV. DISCUSSION

The previous chapter indicates that 38 percent of the respondents lived with or close to children/grandchildren. Most of them also reported their dependency on the latter during periods of crises or need. It thus appears that the older Chinese might be well cared for by their families. Closer examination of the data, however, reveals that a majority of the interviewees identified lack of respect and caring for the aged as a characteristic of the younger generation. They listed the younger people's involvement in their own lives, their giving little time and support to the old folks and not looking after the parents among the complaints. Thus, the issue which superficially can be regarded as a "taking care of one's own" takes a critical turn. Culturally, children are expected to listen to and provide for their aged parents. Our respondents expressed their expectations of their families which perhaps were not being met. Rather than telling the interviewers of the shame and disappointment they might be experiencing, the respondents replied in compliance to the cultural expectations ("no need, my children take care of me"), accounting for the seeming contradiction in the responses.

Use of Formal Assistance as Effected by Cultural Values

Health and language problems appeared to be causing the elderly respondents the most difficulty. Many of them, 48 percent, knew about agencies that provided health and medical care, but only 16 percent had availed themselves of such services. The fact that less than one-half of the respondents (42 percent) could get by speaking English and that even fewer, 32 percent, could read and understand printed forms is a partial explanation for the low utilization of health services. In addition to language barriers, respondents also listed the high cost of medical care (38 percent), distrust of Western medicine (24 percent) and the fear of illness and consequences (14 percent), as factors contributing to the nonuse of services provided by the dominant culture. One might speculate that many of the older people were taking Chinese herbs and medicine at home, or seeing a Chinese doctor rather than going to a Western doctor, although neither MediCal nor Medicare pay for the medicine or the visit.

Coping

Professional and institutional assistance is a relatively new concept to the elderly Chinese. Help that used to come from family, friends and community is not as available now as it was in the village back home. With the families preoccupied with their own lives and community members not helping each other as much, most of the respondents coped with their problems with tolerance. Many of them were probably sincere when they replied that "turning to oneself or no one" in time of need is the practical expectation. For example, almost all respondents stored food in their homes, not only as a matter of convenience but as a safeguard against time of need.

Recognizing the realities of their situation, respondents called for social programs specifically tailored to their needs. They expect social work professionals to possess bilingual and bicultural proficiency and to practice their cultural knowledge. They also consider it important for the professionals to learn about people's needs from outreach and to be courteous and patient.

Employment

Among those sampled, 54 percent of the elderly Chinese voiced no interest in working beyond retirement age. Many had worked long arduous years at low-paying and low-status jobs. Racial discrimination, poor English skills and lacking knowledge of the American society made job advancement extremely difficult. Considering the factors of age and negative work experience, these elderly respondents appeared discouraged about employment beyond retirement, which might offer them relief from their previous hardship.

The younger respondents, however, especially those whose immigration was more recent, demonstrated a relatively higher interest in employment. Some of them wanted to work in order to support themselves, with the hope of qualifying for social security benefits in the future. Unfortunately, the lack of English capability and marketable skills remained obstacles to these expectations.

Residence

Although a large number (86 percent) of the interviewees condidered their neighborhood a good place to live, 36 percent of them indicated a willingness to move if given the opportunity. They wanted to live in closer proximity to friends and family with whom they could communicate. Nearness to members of their own ethnic group is an important factor to survival among older Chinese. If isolated from their own community, many of these people would be doomed to lives of loneliness, devoid of emotional support.

Ethnicity

Every respondent identified himself/herself as Chinese, using their own dialectic term. A 56-year-old respondent, born and raised in America, befriended no Chinese, but protested, "I am Chinese. Heck with those guys that don't think I am!"

Ethnicity is reflected in their lifestyles, as they had mostly Chinese friends (70 percent), and 66 percent belonged to organizations of the same ethnic composition. Of the total sample, 94 percent reported a diet consisting of mostly Chinese food. As many as 68 percent celebrated ethnic festivals and family birthdays by having loved ones for dinner where special festival foods were prepared.

Concept of Aging

"Oldness" was interpreted as a physical and mental condition, but many respondents replied only "chronological age." "Being old is like me" was a common reply. Aging among these elderly Chinese appears to be an acceptable and natural part of living.

"Chinese-ness" Among Older Chinese

Characteristic factors related by the respondents that represent what constitutes "Chinese-ness" follow:

- Expectation of children supporting and helping them in their old age.
- About 90 percent of the sample showed hospitality in offering food and drinks, invitation to meals, giving homegrown or homemade food to interviewers, inviting them to visits again.
- Diet—foreign or American born Chinese (94 percent) both enjoyed Chinese food as regular diet.
- "Clanishness"—forty percent living in neighborhoods with Chinese neighbors. Associations with organizations that were predominantly Chinese, 66 percent.
- Celebration of family happenings with family and friends—birthdays especially—by having big dinners, 68 percent.
- Almost all respondents indicated having food in the house, dried, canned or fresh.
- At least 40 percent had close relatives or immediate family members in the old country. It is more economical for many to support these relatives by sending American dollars back home where the standard of living is much lower. Besides, with immigration already a problematic process, the potential immigrants who often lack salable skills and language proficiency may find adjustment to the American society difficult and discouraging.
- The Chinese calendar is used to calculate age and significant dates.
- Place of birth is identified in terms of village, province, and country.
- Strong identification with own countrymen. People refer to each other in kinship terms especially if they have the same name or speak the same dialect. They might call all older people "grandma" and "grandpa," call people of the same age "brothers" and "sisters" or "uncle" and "aunt," or call younger people "sons" or "daughters." (This is substantiated through observations and not data.)
- All respondents did identify themselves as Chinese, or Chinese in America (regardless of the dialects they speak, the only English term for *Tang* people, Chinese people or *Wah* people is Chinese), even though they might be American born and seldom associate with Chinese.

Brokerage

A majority of the respondents (58 percent), helped their friends, neighbors, family members and church. Their assistance was given for sickness, transportation, financial need and physical chores. The respondents referred to those friends and professionals who helped them as *Yau-Sum* (good-hearted). Those Yau-Sum helpers knew how to help and were willing to do so. They spoke the same dialect and were sincere. Along the same line, the interviewers were also considered service brokers because of their sincerity, knowledge of people and resources, readiness to offer assistance, and their bicultural capabilities.

The interviewers also identified 10 percent of the sample as service-linkage persons. According to their characteristics, these individuals could be grouped into two categories, namely those in authority, and the indigenous service-brokers. The following is a list of characteristics of each group.

Service-linkage persons.

Those persons in authority (ministers, leaders of community) or who hold some kind of office, have the responsibilities of helping others whether or not they are paid for it.

    a. Bilingual, educated
    b. Financially independent
    c. Sociable—enjoy meeting and helping people
    d. Mobile—can drive and own car or know of someone who does
    e. Verbal—not shy about speaking up to defend or fight for a cause
    f. Have good relationship with family and children
    g. Known to community
    h. Healthy, no physical handicaps
    i. Understand changing lifestyles for young and old Chinese in America
    j. Know about resources, people or organizations
    k. Offer help when see need arises

Indigenous service-brokers.

    a. Sociable—enjoy meeting and helping others and eager to help
    b. Attends church or community functions
    c. Mobile—drive or know their way around
    d. May or may not be bilingual—literate, at least in Chinese
    e. Enjoy good relationship with family and children
    f. Accept changing lifestyles for Chinese, young and old, in America
    g. Enjoy good health
    h. Financially independent
    i. Helps friends or groups for births, weddings, birthdays or festivals
    j. Understanding and empathetic
    k. Know about services and may have used them
    l. Would ask for help when needed

Sensitive Areas

It was noted by interviewers that certain areas caused respondents anxiety. The family was a sensitive area, especially for those respondents who had relatives outside of the United States who for political, immigration and/or financial reasons could not be united.

Respondents were also reluctant to disclose the specifics of their financial situation. A round-up monthly income figure (e.g., $200 or $300) was usually given and with hesitance. In most cases, instead of an amount, "just enough" or "enough to meet the expenses" were the responses.

Questions that required probing by the interviewers presented difficulty to 10 percent of the respondents. Those who had little education or did not regard themselves as authorities, were shy and embarrassed by the questions. They reacted by looking down and said meekly, "I don't know, it is too difficult for me," or "It is not for me to say."

Limitations of the Study

Chinese from different parts of China have different customs and speak different dialects. The sample size of 50 in the AoA Study was not big enough to allow detailed comparisons between the two biggest groups from China, namely, the Mandarin-speaking and the Cantonese-speaking. No comparisons were drawn between the American-born Chinese, those who had been in this country for over 50 to 60 years, and the more recent immigrants.

Since the study was conducted in San Diego County, the findings are restricted geographically and to a selected sample of respondents.

Possible Errors in the Questionnaire

A high percentage of the sample knew about MediCal and Medicare. However, relatively few of them had used or were using either benefit. Part of the reasons for this nonuse of service can be accounted for by the fact that both benefits have age 65 and/or financial requirements, which rendered some of our younger and/or better-to-do respondents ineligible.

When asked about their knowledge of formal agencies, many knew only Medicare and MediCal for their health needs, and social security and supplemental security income for financial needs. A majority of them cited their private doctors for medical services. Thus, from the significant percentage of responses, it might appear that the respondents were aware of a variety of public and private social agencies. In reality, however, the elderly knew only of a few governmental programs but were uninformed about community services to which they were also entitled.

V. RECOMMENDATIONS

General Recommendations

The recommendations outlined below are general in nature and are applicable to a variety of individuals and interest groups:

1. Service providers must be flexible and responsive to individuals and group client needs in order to minimize language and cultural barriers;
2. Outreach information must be more explicit and presented from the perspective of the Chinese elderly;
3. Research and service must be more interrelated if meaningful and substantive data are to be obtained. It is essential for researchers to be more aware of services and to be able to provide directions to potential clients when the need arises. It is important to develop a relationship between the information providers and information seekers for the purposes of research if high-quality and substantive information is to be obtained and eventually validated;
4. Federal agencies should develop more effective means of record keeping and data gathering in relation to ethnic older people to ensure that future funding for programs is adequate. The undercount in the census of ethnics and particularly the older populations has tended to leave responsible program agencies with the impression that there is a limited need for services to the minority ethnic populations. It is essential to have adequate and appropriate demographic data in order to provide an awareness for the entitlements;
5. Federal funding sources should seriously consider the feasibility of developing standards for the design and conduct of training programs for community-based minorities who are interested in being involved in research and research implementation and utilization. Currently there is very little training for paraprofessionals in ethnic communities who represent a wealth of untapped manpower and expertise for the purposes of research. The potential is unlimited in that they would provide an entry into the community with an understanding of the norms and cultural concerns as well as technical know-how.
6. Foodstamp facilities and medical programs are often available in the community at large, however, either because of ineffective communication· or language barriers, the services are underutilized by the Chinese elderly;
7. Provisions should be made for technical assistance to be provided to community-based ethnic groups to assist in the design and development of research methodology. Research for and by minorities has more often been weak methodologically than ideologically;
8. There should be particular emphasis on training ethnic researchers who will be able to work as professionals in minority communities and to provide expertise to translate findings about target populations to responsible planners and programmers. They can also provide consistency in research style, utilization of language and develop formal conclusions directly related to the data;
9. Further research should be conducted on the effect of ethnic identification of the utilization of services for the purposes intended;

10. Research should be conducted to determine the extent to which culturalization and socialization have an impact on the awareness and utilization of public or private services. Further work should be done to validate the instruments used in seeking information regarding ethnic older persons;
11. Systematic and ongoing efforts should be made to involve professional researchers, agency leaders, and consumers in research efforts;
12. Agencies should continue to be encouraged to develop systems of accountability which can reflect the inclusion of minority input;
13. All research projects and programs in aging, to the extent possible, should include components to provide more information and data on ethnic older persons;
14. Serious efforts should be made to ensure that there are minority students in research training programs sponsored by federal agencies; and
15. In-service training programs paid for by federal funds should include means of collecting and using data regarding ethnic older people.

The recommendations suggested above are not intended to be exclusive as indicated earlier. They are to serve only as guide for further thinking and action.

Specific Recommendations

Services.

It appears that possession of both bilingual and bicultural capabilities are essential qualities that service providers should have in order to gain trust of the seniors. Training of people with such an ethnic background would enhance the delivery of social services to seniors who need them. Informing minority agencies of future findings and providing them with technical assistance in applying culturally relevant programs is another way governmental departments on various levels can do for the minority aged.

As suggested by the respondents, social work professionals need to possess certain good qualities such as patience, understanding and respect for the elderly. Furthermore, they should be capable and knowledgeable of their profession. Outreach is indicated as an effective way of building trust and communication between the professionals and the seniors.

The study also points out the possibility of training identifiable service brokers in the community to be employed as agency workers.

Research.

From the AoA Study, it appears that bilingual and bicultural researchers best design a research project specific for the ethnic aged. Thus, training of researchers with an ethnic background could enhance the field of social study on the minority elderly population. The AoA Study also demonstrated the great success of training and indigenous ethnic persons to be interviewers, as reflected by the valuable information they reported during the debriefings. Some interviewers proved themselves to be effective service linkage persons during the interviews.

GLOSSARY

Meaning	Calligraphy	Phonetics (Cantonese)
Chinese	中國人	jung gog yun
People from the Dynasty of Tang, most prosperous period in Chinese history, term used by the See Yup speaking	唐 人	tong yun
People from Wah-Ha period before Chinese history was being recorded, from which China developed	華 人	wah yun
"Good Hearted," a term used to describe a service broker who is seen as helpful, knowledgeable about services and respectful towards users	有 心	yau sum
Enthusiastic and contributive toward public cause in describing the service brokers	熱 心	yit sum
Incompetent, in describing professionals who cannot communicate with clients, ignorant about helping people, impatient and rude	無 用	mo yung
Not much good, in describing themselves in old age, a humble expression, rather than what it literally means, reflecting their inability to do a lot of things they did when younger	無 用	mo yung
Be nice to older people, taking care of them and listening to their advice	尊 敬	june ging
Follow the parents' advice, support them in old age, visit them often	孝 敬	how ging

Offer the necessary assistance if you can when your fellowman is in trouble, e.g., counseling—talking to attempt to solve problems—, physical help—cooking babysitting, making clothes

互相幫助   wo seung bong jor

Transportation, driving others to where they have to go in own car

Interpretation/translation, because of their bilingual capabilities

Don't need formal assistance; expect their children to take care of them

Minority or colored, the respondents referred to the black and brown people as such, but not themselves. The terms appeared to carry a negative connotation to the elderly who identified themselves as Chinese

In talking about how they were being treated in the United States in the past, some English-speaking respondents referred to themselves and other groups from Asia as Orientals rather than Asians

Medicare and Social Security benefits were not regarded as services by the respondents. Instead, these programs were considered something they earned and paid into before they retired. The government was just saving their tax dollars for the retirement benefits. Other services were thought of as charity or depending on strangers.

/E. Cheng|

Methodological References

Alvarez, Rudolfo. The unique psychohistorical experience of the Mexican American people. *Social Science Quarterly,* 1971, *52* (1), 12-29.

Blauner, Robert, & Wellman, David. Toward the decolonization of social research. In Joyce A. Laher (Ed.) *The death of white sociology.* New York: Vintage Books, 1973.

Campbell, Donald T., & Stanley, Julian. *Experimental and quasi experimental designs for research.* Chicago: Rand McNally College Publishing Co., 1963.

Clark, Margaret, & Anderson, Barbara Gallatin. *Culture and aging: An anthropological study of the older American.* Springfield, Ill.: Charles C. Thomas, 1967.

Cooley, Charles H. Primary groups. In Paul H. Hare, Edgar F. Borgutta, & Robert F. Bales (Eds.) *Small groups: Studies in social interaction.* New York: Alfred A. Knopf, 1955.

Counting the forgotten: The 1970 census count of persons of Spanish-speaking background in the United States. Washington, D.C.: U.S. Government Printing Office, 1974.

Federal Register. Title 45: public welfare, Part 46: protection of human subjects, 1975, *40* (50), 11854-11858.

García, Ernest. Chicano Spanish dialects and education. *Aztlan,* 1971, *2* (1), 67-73.

Glaser, Barney G., & Straus, Anselom L. *The discovery of grounded theory.* Chicago: Aldine Publishing Co., 1967.

Gouldner, Alvin (Ed.). Explorations in applied social science. In Alvin W. Gouldner, & S.M. Miller (Eds.) *Applied sociology opportunities and problems.* New York: The Free Press, 1965.

Hamilton, Charles. Black social scientists: Contributions and problems. In Joyce Ladner (Ed.) *The death of white sociology.* New York: Vintage Books, 1973.

Lofland, John. *Analyzing social settings.* Belmont, Pennsylvania: Wadsworth Publishing Co., Inc., 1974.

Moore, Joan W. Situational factors affecting minority aging. *Gerontologist,* 1971, *2* (2), 88-93.

——————————. Social constraints on sociological knowledge: academics and research concerning minorities. *Social Problems,* 1973, *21* (1), 65-77.

Murase, Kenji. Ethnic minority content in the social work curriculum: Social welfare policy and social research. In *Perspectives on ethnic minority content in social work education.* Boulder, Colo.: Western Interstate Commission for Higher Education, 1972.

Romano, Octavio. The historical and intellectual presence of Mexican Americans. *El Grito,* 1969, *2* (2), 13-26.

Sieber, Sam D. The integration of field work and survey methods. *American Journal of Sociology,* 1973, *48,* 1335-1359.

Solomon, Barbara. Growing old in the ethnosystem. In E. Percil Stanford (Ed.) *Minority aging: Proceedings of the Institute on Minority Aging.* San Diego: The Campanile Press, San Diego State University, 1974.

Stebbins, Robert A.   The unstructured research interview as interpersonal relationship. *Sociology and Social Research,* 1972, 56, 164-179.

Takagi, Paul.   The myth of "assimilation in American life." *Amerasia Journal,* 1973, 2, 149-158.

Truzzi, Marcello (Ed.).   *Verstehen, subjective understanding in the social sciences.* Reading, Mass.: Addison, Wesley Publishing Co., 1974.

Vaca, Nick C.   The Mexican American in the social sciences, 1912-1970, part I. *El Grito,* 1970, *1* (1), 53-78.

_____. The Mexican American in the social sciences, 1912-1970, part II. *El Grito,* 1970, *3* (3), 3-24.

Valle, Ramón.   *Amistad-compadrazgo as an indigenous webwork, compared with the urban mental health network.* Unpublished doctoral dissertation, University of Southern California, 1974.

Webb, Eugene; Campbell Donald; Schwartz, Richard; & Schrest, Lee.   *Unobstrusive measures: Non-reactive research in the social sciences.* Chicago: Rand-McNally Co., 1971.

Appendix A
The Chinese Experience in the United States

Review of the Literature

The arrival of large numbers of Chinese pioneers to the shores of California in the 1850s signaled the beginning of the first large-scale migration of a free, non-white people to the United States. It also marked the third effort at labor recruitment to work the land laid open by European explorers and entrepreneurs. The first effort was the impressment of Native Americans, the second the importation of African slaves. Both efforts were unsuccessful due to resistance of the Native Americans and anti-slavery sentiment of the West. (Saxton, 1971)

The critical element in the meeting of white and yellow races in California was the confrontation of two societies at different phases of their historical development. With the entrance of Chinese to California, a large industrializing capitalistic democracy confronted the peasant class and the merchant class of the strife-torn, agrarian China. The confrontation resulted in cultural, economical, racial and institutional conflicts which make up another chapter in the history of this country of immigrants.

It is only recently that the story of the Chinese immigrants is being recounted and analyzed in a non-stereotypical fashion. Based on Dr. Harry Kitano's *Asian Americans: An Annotated Bibliography* and library research, one can categorize the writings on this subject into four general approaches. The first category includes writings that have contributed to or are perpetuating the stereotypes of Chinese. These writings began to appear as early as 1885, proliferated mostly through newspapers, and they persist to the present day. Examples are lengthy chapters on "heathen" conditions in China and Chinatown, detailed maps of various houses of "vice" in Chinatown (Farwell, 1885), history and lengthy discussions of opium dens (Asbury, 1933). When giving a character sketch of the Chinese people, the author chooses a humble, happy Chinese cook (Dickson, 1957), and describes foot binding as a "curious, erotic, custom" (Levy, 1964). Perhaps the most illustrative writing to characterize this category of writing is the book *Pigtails and Goldust*, which uses every stereotyped theme that early literature and later movies were to touch upon. Witness the author's opening remark:

> This volume was evolved with the idea of recording the trials and tribulations of a fast-fading picture of the most romantic figures of far Western history—the pig-tailed Chinaman—the story of his opium dens, slave girls, Joss Houses and Tong Wars. (McLeod, 1974:8)

The second category includes writings with a journalistic approach, travel logs, guide books and some relatively more sensitive writings about Chinatowns and their customs. This category in general, also perpetuates the stereotypes, but did not exploit them to the same degree as those mentioned in the previous category.

The third category of writings includes serious historical and sociological studies of the Chinese American experience. These writings are authored by both Anglo Americans and Chinese Americans. The degree of depth of understanding and appreciativeness varies with the authors. One example of the differing degree of appreciativeness shown in the literature is the comparison of Gunther Barth and Victor Nee. On the subject of acculturation, a comparison of these two authors' remarks reveal very different points of reference:

> The [Chinese laborers] had left home and entered into a life of bondage in defense of the tenets of their culture. Consequently, they rejected values [Anglo American] which undermined the meaning of their plight. (Barth, 1964:157)

Bitter Strength, the book from which the above remark is extracted, presented a well documented and analyzed history of the Chinese American experience. It is, however, definitely perceived from an Anglo-majority point of view, in that the discussion did not include an analysis of the strength that is expressed in the rejection and the acknowledgement that rejection was on both sides. Victor and Brett Nee in *Longtime Californ'* expressed the other view.

> Excluded from participation in American political, social and economic life..., Chinatown by the turn of the century had developed within itself a complicated organized network to answer the vital needs of its population.... By reinforcing its cohesiveness within, and buffering it from hostile forces outside, they [the organizations] have been an important source of the exceptional resilience and continuity of the community. (Nee and Nee, 1972:63-64)

The fourth category of writings concerning the Chinese American experience is the literary novels, poetry and plays. This category can be separated into two distinct types of authors by their identity with and lack of identity with the Chinese community in America. The latter utilized the Chinese American experience as a background or insight into some literary purposes. The former perceived themselves as the literary voices of the Chinese American community and have strong identity with it.

Early records of Chinese pioneers in America during the late 1700s revealed the Chinese immigrants as mostly crewmen, domestic servants of missionaries and travelers, merchants, students and entertainers in the circus. The arrival of Chinese from the south seaport of Kwangtung Province to the shores of California in significant numbers occurred in the 1850s. It was a movement that is closely ties in with the political strife and economic breakdown in China and the need for cheap labor by the developers of the western United States.

Over 95 percent of the Chinese in American came from Kwangtung Province in the south of China (of them, 70 percent are from the Sae Yup District), a province that ranked seventh in population and yet ranked third lowest in acreage of agricultural land per capita. China in 1850 was emerging from a decade of defeat. The British victory in the Opium War (1840-1842) and the First Unequal Treaties had thrown the ruling Manchu Dynasty into crisis and had opened China to the penetration of Western imperialist powers for the next century. Compounding the foreign aggressions, China was torn internally by the Taiping Rebellion (an estimated million persons were killed in Kwangtung Province) and the Triad Uprising in the Pearl River Delta, the main river in Kwangtung. The economic basis of the region was shaken, and young men sought financial resources overseas.

By 1860, 34,933 Chinese were in the United States, nearly all in California and represented slightly more than 9 percent of all Californians. The majority residing in California had joined the gold rush in the foothills to work out low-yield digs and the abandoned tailing in order to avoid competition and eviction by the white miners. As the mines were finally giving out, from 1866 to 1869, the Chinese labor composed nine out of ten workers in the Central Pacific Railroad workforce. Afterwards, a small percentage of Chinese stayed to build railroads within California while the majority went into the valley to fill the enormous agricultural labor demand for clearing, ditching, draining, irrigating the swampy land of the valley and harvesting the new crops. In analyzing the Chinese labor question, Saxton, a noted labor historian, remarked:

> Viewing the state as a whole, then, Chinese were found in occupations which required little or no skills, in occupations stigmatized as menial and in manufacturing. In a general way, the division between Chinese and non-Chinese corresponded to lives of skill or prestige. (Saxton, 1972)

Demobilization and postwar recession, followed by the opening of the railroad, brought a westward migration of working men from the East Coast. That was the setting of the Anti-Chinese Movement in the West. Traditionally, the anti-Chinese sentiment, at that time, was analyzed as the result of the clash of the cultural and institutional differences. Historians (Miller and Barth) persuasively argue that the hostility toward the Chinese, which finally resulted in the Exclusion Law of 1882, was due to the threat of cheap Coolie (苦力 Ku-li) labor to the labor class of this country and represented the conflict between the capitalists who hire slaves and sojourners and the labor class that was struggling to establish decent wages. New light has been shed on this problem in terms of the additional factor of political and economic racism in America's labor history (Saxton, Nee, Wu). Victor and Brett de Barry Nee documented in their book one of their theses, "While it is true that the cultural, economic and institutional gulf between Chinese and American Californians was great, it is euphemistic to ignore the persistent definition of Chinese as non-white races" (Nee, 1972, p. 32). One cannot dismiss as mere coincidence the often-made parallel in the press of the Anti-Chinese Movement era between "Niggers and Chinamen" (Jones, 1955, p. 31). Such statements as, "We want White people to enrich the country, not Mongolians to degrade and disgrace it" (Allport, 1958, p. 185) made by prominent Irish editors, clearly advocated for a racial rather than an ethnic discrimination basis for American immigration policy. The significance of being non-white in America has been a theme in many studies and analyses since the 1960s.

The Chinese Exclusion Act of 1882 as the first law to restrict immigration of an entire ethnic group suspended immigration of Chinese laborers for ten years, forbade Chinese to become naturalized citizens and denied reentry to any Chinese laborers who departed from the United States. The Exclusion Act had the single most significant role in shaping the Chinese community in America. The following census chart from 1860-1970 shows the Chinese American population as corresponding to the enactment of the Act and the repeal of the Act in 1943.

Chinese-American Population 1860-1970

Year	Population	Ratio Women:Men
1860	34,933	100:1859
1870	63,199	—
1880	105,465	—
1890	107,488	—
1900	89,863	100:1887
1910	71,331	—
1920	61,639	100:695
130	74,954	—
1940	77,504	—
1950	117,629	—
1960	237,293	100:135
1970	435,062	100:100

Legislation such as Foreign Miners' Tax Law of 1850, Capitation Tax Law of 1855 and Police Tax Law of 1862 which levied taxes on Chinese in America, are legal expressions of the anti-Chinese sentiment which was often expressed in illegal, violent acts. They are the forerunners of the Exclusion Act. The sixty years of exclusion had shaped the structure of Chinese communities in America and the lifestyle of this generation of Chinese American senior citizens. The Exclusion Act has created a bachelor society for the Chinese in America. They are the lonely old men we see today playing chess in Portsmouth Square in San Francisco, Chinatown and living in deteriorated rooms in downtown hotels in every metropolitan area. The Exclusion Act separated families and prevented marriages. Most sojourners led lonely bachelor lives in an almost all-male society. They came when there was no more gold to be dug, no more railroad to be laid; all that remained was the experience of the treatment as an "exempted class" — being placed in detention sheds on Angel Island in San Francisco Bay upon arrival in the United States for days, months and even years of questioning; being demanded constantly of papers; being in a community that was often raided for illegals; being a migrant farm worker; being a servant (documented in Lai, 1973). The tactics of immigration officers resulted in Chinese immigrants viewing governmental officials as objects of fear and symbols of oppression. It also strengthened the internal protective structures within Chinese communities. The clan-village as a basic economic unit structure which existed in villages in Kwantung, was useful again for the same reason—survival. Strong family ties, a traditional value, is almost unnatural for sojourners, who at best saw their families three or four times in their lifetimes and perhaps rejoined them after forty years of separation and at worst, never united with the family again. With no hope of the family over (due to the Exclusion Act), the original purpose of the sojourner to make good and go home to better the family fortune was a dream that never came true. With no hope of marriage in the United States (due to the anti-miscegenation laws, 1906-1948), there was no alternative but to retain the broken pieces of a dream.

The history of Chinese in America is the root of today's Chinese community in America. For this generation of Chinese American elderly, the history describes their youth.

Selected Bibliography on the Chinese Experience in the United States

Allport, G.   The nature of prejudice. New York: Addison-Wesley, 1954.

Asbury, H.   The Barbary Coast. New York: Knopf, 1933.

Dickson, S.   Tales of San Francisco. Palo Alto: Stanford University Press, 1957.

Farwell, F.B.   The Chinese at home and abroad. San Francisco: A.L. Bancroft, 1885.

Jones, D.   The portrayal of China and India on the American screne. Cambridge, Mass.: [n.p.], 1955.

Kitano, H.; Jung, E.; Tanaka, C.; & Wong, B.   Asian American: An annotated bibliography. New York: Council on Social Work Education, 1971.

Lai, H., & Choy, P.P.   Outline history of the Chinese in America. San Francisco: Chinese American Studies Planning Group, 1973.

Levy, H.   Chinese footbinding: The history of a curious erotic custom. New York: Twayne, 1964.

McLeod, A.   Pigtails and goldust. Idaho: Caxton Printers, 1947.

Miller, S.C.   The unwelcome immigrant. Berkeley and Los Angeles: University of California Press, 1969.

Nee, V.G., & Nee, B.deB.   Longtime Californ'. New York: Pantheon Books, 1972.

Saxton, A.   The indispensable enemy. Berkeley and Los Angeles: University of California Press, 1971.

Wu, Cheng-Tsu. Chink. New York: World Publishing, 1972.

LITERATURE ON PACIFIC AND ASIAN AMERICAN ELDERLY

The annotated bibliography that follows is a listing of literature on Asian American elderly. The books and articles are mostly about the elderly in the Chinese, Japanese and Filipino communities and none on the elderly Guamanian. It is made part of this section for the substantive information they provide, the conceptual views of aging among Asian Americans and the generalizations that may be derived for perspectives on the elderly Guamanian. Kalish and Moriwaki suggest that older Americans share a great deal with their fellow Asian Americans and with their fellow elderly, but that there is a personal history and present milieu that is shared neither with younger persons of similar national origin nor with age cohorts of various national origins; and that understanding these individuals requires knowledge of their cultural origins and effects of early socialization, their life history in the United States, those age-related changes that occur regardless of early learning or ethnicity, and their expectations as to what it means to be old (1973, p. 190).

While these books and articles are valuable in the search for a firm foundation from which to view aging among the Asian American elderly, they also reflect the near absence of literature on tested programmatic assumptions and their efficacy for planners and programmers. Planners, programmers, and theoreticians alike struggle with the stark reality of the overwhelming effects of racism, inaccessbility of resources, and the lack of community-based services which force many older Asians to live in poverty. The readings should provide some information on cultural variables as related to problems of old age, poverty, poor health, language barrier, and insular existence of the elderly Asian Americans. To the extent that this bibliography encourages students of social gerontology to inquire, and the curiosity that it may generate about the elderly Asian and Pacific islander, the work of the compilers seems justified.

ANNOTATED BIBLIOGRAPHY ON
PACIFIC AND ASIAN AMERICAN ELDERLY

Books

Abbott, Kenneth A.   *Cultural change, psychological functioning and the family: A case study in the Chinese American community of San Francisco.*   Ann Arbor: University of Michigan, 1971.

A study of cultural change among Chinese American families in San Francisco. A lengthy sociological study of Chinese norms and values and their effects on psychological functioning.

Bessent, T.E.   An aging Issei anticipates rejection. In G. Seward (Ed.) *Clinical studies in cultural conflict.*   New York: Ronald Press, 1958.

The case study discusses an older Japanese American man who had entered a State Mental Hospital. The patient's diagnosis is viewed with relationship to cultural variables. The study provides a clinical perspective for understanding the behavior of an older Japanese man.

Kiefer, Christie W.   *Changing cultures, changing lives: An ethnographic study of three generations of Japanese Americans.*   San Francisco: Jossey-Bass, 1975.

The ethnographic study of the Japanese American community in San Francisco is a cross-cultural study of personality throughout the life cycle. It views personality as a life-long process that dynamically interacts with cultural and historical change. Older Japanese Americans are discussed with relationship to attitudes toward them, their dependency needs, morals, grandparent roles, services provided them, etc.

Kitano, Harry H.L.   *Japanese Americans: The evolution of a subculture.*   Englewood Cliffs: Prentice-Hall, Inc., 1969.

Kitano traces the evolution of Japanese Americans as a subculture group. The discussion of Issei is most relevant to Asian aging. The Issei are first-generation Americans in the over-70 age bracket. They remain Japanese oriented and have continued in their old ways, conforming, hard-working, group and family oriented, clinging to old values, customs and goals. The Issei have found a fairly satisfying way of life. Many live with or close to their families. They define their success in terms of the success of their children.

Articles and Journals

Berk, Bernard B., & Hirata, Lucie C.   Mental illness among the Chinese: Myth or reality? *Journal of Social Issues,* 1973, *29* (2), 149-166.

The article examines trends in mental hospital commitments among Chinese in California over the past 100 years. There has been a two-fold increase among Chinese in California. Males, the aged, and the foreign born experienced significantly higher rates of commitment than did the Chinese American population as a whole.

Boyd, Monica.   The Chinese in New York, California, and Hawaii. *Phylon,* 1971, *32* (2), 1.

A socioeconomic study of Chinese males by age residing in New York, California, and Hawaii. Comparisons are presented on industrial classification, occupational categories, educational attainment, median income, percentage of foreign born, and percentage with spouse absent but not legally separated. Depicts differences in occupation and socioeconomic characteristics of foreign born and native Chinese.

Kalish, Richard A., & Moriwaki, Sharon.   The world of the Asian American. *Journal of Social Issues,* 1973, *29* (2), 187-209.

The Asian American's appearance, language, value system, and rules of behavior are different from other groups. Filial piety ranks higher in Eastern cultures, and the Asian American expects to be rewarded for past accomplishments, but this failed to happen in the United States. Few services are offered in their communities, so when they need help the aged have to leave their communities. They then become isolated and fearful, being cut off from familiar food, language, and values.

Kalish, Richard A., & Yuen, Sam.   Americans of East Asian ancestry: Aging and the aged. *Gerontologist,* 1971, *11* (1:2), 36-47.

The selection considers the three largest groupings from East Asia (Chinese American, Japanese American, Filipino American). Although these groups have similarities, they are distinctly different in their traditions, their language, their religion, and their history in the United States. The article studies these groups in relation to background, statistical descriptive data, current research, and directions for future research.

Masuda, Minary; Matsumoto, Gary H.; & Meredith, Gerald M.   Ethnic identity in three generations of Japanese Americans. *Journal of Social Psychology*, 1970, *81*, 199-207.

Three generations of Japanese Americans were studied (Issei, Nisei, and Sansei). There was a gradual erosion of ethnicity as acculturation proceeded. Sex was not a significant factor in ethnic identification, but age, education, occupational prestige, and religion appeared to have some relevance. Ethnic identification as a factor in current behavior, values, attitudes, and personality of Japanese Americans is discussed.

Modell, John.   The Japanese American family. *The Pacific Historical Review*, 1968, *37*, 67-81.

The article contends that the history of the Issei generation can be understood only by recognizing that: (1) ocean-spanning, many generational family has served the Issei as a durable social institution, (2) Issei were under extreme emotional pressure to believe that this institution constituted a moral as well as a biological continuity between the generation of their fathers and their sons.

Wu, Frances Y.   Mandarin-speaking aged Chinese in the Los Angeles area. *Gerontologist*, 1975, *15* (3), 271-275.

The study indicated that the Mandarin-speaking elderly are the victims of political, social, economic, and cultural changes, including the change in the concept of filial piety. Inability to speak or understand English was the most serious problem for the elderly, who immigrated at an old age. Language barrier and culture shock alienated the Chinese from the mainstream of American society, and excluded them from receiving needed services.

Yuen, Sam.   Aging and mental health in San Francisco's Chinatown. *Ethnicity, Mental Health, and Aging*. Los Angeles: Ethel Percy Andrus Gerontology Center, University of Southern California, 1970.

The article discusses current living conditions in Chinatown in San Francisco. In addition, some information is given about the culture brought by the original immigrants. Today, poverty, old age, poor health, and discrimination all contribute to the immobilization of the older Chinese American in the ghetto community. There is a widening gap between generations, resulting in less value being placed on the elderly. The author suggests strategies for intervention.

Documents

The Asian American elderly.   (Reports of the Special Concerns Sessions, 1971 White House Conference on Aging.) Washington, D.C.: U.S. Government Printing Office, 1971.

The report delineates the major problems facing older Asian Americans in the United States. It clarifies needed areas for research and the development of services. Further, it designates specific areas where Federal policy should be developed to meet the needs of the Asian elderly.

Californians of Japanese, Chinese, and Filipino ancestry: Population, employment, income, education. San Francisco: State of California, Department of Industrial Relations, Division of Fair Employment Practices, June 1965.

The document provides demographic data on Japanese, Chinese, and Filipino Californians in the following areas: population, place of birth, area of residence, educational attainment, industry distribution, occupations, unemployment, income, and size of family. The accuracy of the data should be viewed in relation to date of publication. It provides a good background for studying the Asian community.

On the feasibility of training Asians to work with Asian elderly: A preliminary assessment of needs and resources available to Asian elderly in Seattle, Washington—training project for the Asian elderly. March 1973.

The report is a comprehensive overview of the Asian American elderly in the Seattle, Washington area. The document provides a survey of the needs of the elderly Asian American, an assessment of the needs of the elderly by Asian community leaders, a survey of social service agencies serving the elderly, and resources within the Asian community available to the elderly. The underlying purpose of the document was to provide guidelines for training Asian Americans to provide services to the Asian elderly.

Profile: Oahu's senior citizens. City and County of Honolulu's Office of Human Resources, July 1973.

The document provides basic demographic and labor-force data concerning Oahu's aged population. The information is based primarily upon the 1970 United States Census and the Hawaii State Department of Health's 1969-1971 Surveillance Program. The report is organized into four major sections: Population Characteristics, Income and Poverty Status, Employment Characteristics, and the Needs of the Aged.

Other Works

Fujii, Sharon M.   *An exploratory-descriptive study of socio-cultural barriers to health services utilization for elderly Japanese as perceived by middle aged and elderly Japanese Americans.* Unpublished doctoral dissertation, Brandeis University, 1975.

The study explored and described the problem of utilizing health services by elderly Japanese Americans in terms of specific socio-cultural barriers: cultural traditions, the expectation of racial discrimination, alternative ethnic services, and awareness. Findings suggested that all of the presumed socio-cultural barriers to health service utilization affecting elderly Japanese were not necessarily perceived as such by the sample and that only sex significantly differentiated perceptions of the racial discrimination.

Kiefer, Christie W.   *The limitations of theory: A case report on the Japanese American elderly.* (Human Development Program.) San Francisco, California: University of California, 1974.

The report introduces instances of how history and culture complicate the explanation of the Issei adaptation. The Issei case is seen as an example of the limitations of both practical and theoretical knowledge. The article is a complex theoretical discussion that gives insight into future directions in research.

Reynolds, David K.   *Japanese American aging: A game perspective.* Paper presented at the Society for Applied Anthropology Meeting, Miami, Florida, April 15, 1971.

The author focuses on intrafamilial aspects of the Japanese American aging game, which is primarily played out in family setting with family members as the key players. The Issei learned the aging game in Meiji, Japan. Yet the Neisi grew up in a culture with different rules, players, and effective strategies. Four brief cases illustrate degrees of winning and losing the aging game.

ADDITIONAL BIBLIOGRAPHY

Articles

Bogardus, E.S.   Filipino immigrant attitudes. *Sociology and Social Research*, 1930, *14*, 469-479.

Catapusan, B.T.   Leisure time problems of Filipino immigrants. *Sociology of Social Research*, 1940, *24*, 541-549.

Caudill, W., & Scarr, H.A.   Japanese value orientations and cultural changes. *Ethnology*, 1962, *1*, 53-91.

Chandler, Albert R.   The traditional Chinese attitude toward old age. *Journal of Gerontology*, 1949, *4*, 239-244.

Modell, John.   The Japanese American family: a perspective for future investigations. *Pacific Historical Review*, 1968, *36*, 67-81.

Rojo, F.A.   Social maladjustment among Filipinos in the United States. *Sociology and Social Research*, 1937, *21*, 447-457.

Unpublished Material

Chen, W.C.   *Changing socio-cultural patterns of the Chinese community in Los Angeles.* Unpublished doctoral dissertation, University of Southern California, 1952.

Cho, C.S.   *Correlation of cultural assimilation of two groups of Issei women.* Unpublished master's thesis, University of Washington, Seattle, 1953.

Collins, Bill, & Yee, Donna.   *Social forces within the Seattle Filipino American community today: 1972.* Seattle, Washington: Demonstration Project for Asian Americans, February 1972.

Kanaguawa, W.Y.   *A study of old-age assistance recipients of Japanese ancestry under Honolulu County Department of Welfare.* Unpublished master's thesis, University of Hawaii, Honolulu, 1955.

Kimura, Y.   *A comparative study of the collective adjustment of the Issei: The first generation Japanese in Hawaii and in mainland United States since Pearl Harbor.* Unpublished doctoral dissertation, University of Chicago, 1952.

Lee, David Y.   *Report on Korean American community in Los Angeles.* Los Angeles: Demonstration Project for Asian Americans, January 1972.

Marian, H.   *The Filipino immigrant in the United States.* Unpublished master's thesis, University of Chicago, 1934.

On the feasibility of training Asians to work with Asian elderly: A preliminary assessment of needs and resources available to Asian elderly in Seattle, Wahington. Glenn Chinn, Principal Investigator, prepared by Training Project for the Asian Elderly, March 1973.

Ross, R. Social distance between first and second generation Japanese in Los Angeles. Unpublished master's thesis, University of Southern California, 1939.

Stanford, P.S. Values of some Issei Japanese of Hanapepe Valley, Kauai. Unpublished doctoral dissertation, Mississippi State University, State College, 1970.

Tamura, Fumi Yoshida. A cross-generational study of the attitudes toward the aging person and aging process and the acceptance of a "home for the aged" in the Japanese American family. Unpublished master's thesis, University of California, Los Angeles, 1969.

Vanagita, Uiki. Familial, occupational, and social characteristics of three generations of Japanese Americans. Unpublished master's thesis, University of Southern California, 1968.